Prentzas, G. S.
   Tribal law / Scott Prentzas ; series editor, Jordan E.
Kerber. --Vero Beach, Fla. : Rourke Publications,
c1994.
   64 p. : ill. (some col.). --(Native American culture)

Includes bibliographical references (p. 59) and index.
768560 LC: 94005531 ISBN:0866255362 (lib.

(SEE NEXT CARD)
230   97JUN05   3559/ex   1-448039

NATIVE * AMERICAN * CULTURE

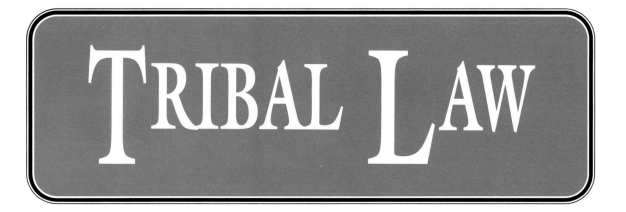

TRIBAL LAW

Scott Prentzas

Series Editor
Jordan E. Kerber, Ph.D.

✳ ✳ ✳

ROURKE PUBLICATIONS, INC.
Vero Beach, Florida 32964

©1994 by Rourke Publications, Inc.

Printed in the United States of America.

A Blackbirch Graphics book.

Library of Congress Cataloging-in-Publication Data

Prentzas, G. S.
Tribal law / by Scott Prentzas.
     p. cm. — (Native American culture)
     Includes bibliographical references and index.
     ISBN 0-86625-536-2
     1. Indians of North America—Legal status, laws, etc.—Juvenile litera-
ture. 2. Indian courts—United States—Juvenile literature. [1. Indians of
North America—Legal status, laws, etc.] I. Title. II. Series.
KF8220.Z9P74   1994
306.2—dc20   94-5531
                                                                  CIP
                                                                   AC

Contents

Introduction

The words "Native Americans" and "Indians" create strong images for many people. Some may think of fierce warriors with bows and arrows, tomahawks, and rifles who battled the U.S. Cavalry in the days of the Wild West. Others probably imagine a proud and peaceful people who just hunted buffalo and lived in tipis on the Great Plains. These are just some of the popular stereotypes of Native Americans, and like most stereotypes they give a false impression.

This series on *Native American Culture* presents six books on various aspects of Native American life: child rearing, arts and crafts, daily life, tribal law, spiritual life, and the invasion by Europe. By reading these books, you will learn that there is no single Native American culture, but instead many different ones. Each Native American group or tribe in the past, as well as today, is a separate nation. While tribes may share some similarities, many are as different from one another as the English are from the Spanish.

The geographic focus of this series is the North American continent (United States and Canada), with special attention to the area within the present-day United States. However, Native Americans have lived, and continue to live, in Central America and South America. In addition, the authors of each book draw upon a wealth of historical information mainly from a time between the 1500s and 1900s, when most Native Americans were first contacted by European explorers, conquerors, and settlers. Much is known

✳

5

about this period of Native American life from documents and observations recorded by Europeans who came to North America.

It is also important to understand that Native Americans have a much longer and more complex history on the continent than just the past 500 years. Archaeologists have excavated ancient Native American sites as old as 12,000 years. The people who lived at these sites were among the first residents of North America. They did not keep written records of their lives, so the only information known about them comes from their stone tools and other remains that they left behind. We do know that during the thousands of years of Native American settlement across the continent the cultures of these early inhabitants changed in many important ways. Some of these cultures disappeared a long time ago, while others have survived and continue to change today. Indeed, there are more than 1.5 million Native Americans currently living in the United States, and the federal government recognizes over 500 tribes. Native Americans are in all walks of life, and many still practice traditions and speak the languages of their ancestors. About 250,000 Native Americans presently live on some 278 reservations in the country.

The books in this series capture the wonderful richness and variety of Native American life from different time periods. They remind us that the story of America begins with Native Americans. They also provide more accurate images of Native Americans, images that I hope will enable you to challenge the stereotypes.

Jordan E. Kerber, Ph.D.
Director of Native American Studies
Colgate University

Chapter

1

Rules of Behavior

Opposite:
Native Americans
built many different
types of homes across the
continent. Here, the
Cliff Palace ruins in
Colorado's Mesa Verde
National Park were
once home to the
Anasazi tribe.

During the Ice Age, which started about 2.5 million years ago and ended more than 11,000 years ago, the water level of the oceans was often very low. At these times, the continents of Asia and North America were connected by a land bridge that stretched between what are now Russia and Alaska. In some places, the land bridge was 1,000 miles across. Today, it lies underneath the waters of the Bering Sea. Scientists believe that the ancestors of Native Americans came to North America as many as 12,000 years ago. They traveled across the land bridge by foot.

By the time European explorers first arrived in the Americas in the 1490s, about 600 different Native American groups—commonly known as tribes—were spread out across the entire continent. These groups lived in many different types of environments, from forests in the East and grasslands on the Great Plains, to deserts in the Southwest and beaches along the Pacific Coast. Each one of these tribes was unique and had its own language, beliefs, and customs. (Customs are ways of acting that have become accepted by a particular society.)

The size of the different tribes also varied. Some Native Americans lived in small bands that hunted buffalo and other large mammals. These bands, such as the Sioux, set up camps as they followed animal herds. Other Native Americans were part of larger tribes, such as the Hopi, that lived in villages and grew crops in nearby fields. Still others were members of large nations, such as the Iroquois, that controlled vast territories.

Native Americans created ways of life that were successful for them. Unfortunately, their communities were soon torn apart. Explorers from England, France, Spain, Holland, and Russia claimed parts of North America for their homeland. Beginning in the 1500s, European settlers began to pour into the continent, overwhelming the native peoples. Native Americans eventually lost most of their land to the settlers. Disease, war, and starvation killed off entire tribes and nearly destroyed the ones that survived.

The settlers disapproved of many Native American customs because they were so unlike their own. These settlers tried to make Native Americans give up their traditional ways of life. Missionaries converted many tribes to Christianity. Schools taught Native American children to think and act like non-Native Americans. In addition, government agencies, such as the Bureau of Indian Affairs, adopted many policies that destroyed tribal customs.

Even though millions of Native Americans throughout North America had governed themselves for thousands of years, non-Native Americans saw them as being lawless

people. The tribes appeared to have no legal systems. They
had no legislatures, no written laws, no courts, no judges,
no police, and no jails. Coming from countries ruled by
kings and queens, Europeans mistakenly thought that tribal
chiefs acted as monarchs and that their word was law.

For many years, these settlers continued to think that
Native Americans had no laws, or rules of behavior. In the
nineteenth century, however, anthropologists began study-
ing Native American societies. They examined tools and
other objects that Native Americans had made in the past.
These anthropologists also visited tribes, observing how
people lived their daily lives and asking elders questions
about traditional ways. Using this information, they then
tried to piece together how Native Americans lived before
the arrival of Europeans.

Anthropologists have studied many aspects of Native
American culture, such as religion, art, and family structure.
Some anthropologists have looked at how tribes dealt with
crimes and disputes between people. They discovered that
Native American tribes did indeed have very effective legal
systems. However, their legal traditions were different from
those of the United States and Europe.

Traditional Native American Law

All societies define the differences between right and wrong,
and all have rules of behavior for individuals to obey. These
rules of behavior can come from many sources, including
religion, customs, and laws. Each society has its own way
of making rules and punishing those who break them.

Native Americans lived without formal legislatures that
passed laws, and without law enforcement agencies. Yet
their societies worked extremely well. Many of the legal
traditions of Native Americans have been lost forever because
they were not recorded, and very little is known about some

tribes. However, anthropologists have learned about some Native American legal traditions.

In most tribes, the family and the community were the center of a person's life. The welfare of the individual often depended on the success of the entire tribe. Everyone was expected to cooperate and to behave in a way that benefited the whole community. No one wanted to lose the respect of his or her family and friends by acting selfishly or disrupting the harmony of the tribe. In general, a tribe's rules of behavior were understood and accepted by all its members.

An Eskimo family in Alaska in 1886. The family unit was a very important part of all Native American tribal societies.

Until the early 1800s, most Native Americans had no written languages. Tribal history and literature were handed down from one generation to the next by word of mouth. Spoken stories taught young people the tribe's customs, beliefs, and values. These tales contained moral lessons that helped people solve problems and get along with each other.

Most Native American tribes were highly democratic. Tribal decisions were made by consensus, which meant that a final decision would be made only when everyone in the tribe was in agreement. Many chiefs and other tribal leaders were not strong rulers. They were usually elected, and their powers were limited. Chiefs offered advice, tried to resolve disputes, and worked to carry out the wishes of the tribe. Before taking action, chiefs usually sought the wisdom and support of tribal elders. (A few tribes had powerful rulers who were very much like the kings and queens of Europe. In those tribes, the ruler's orders were law.)

Crime, as we know it today, was rare among Native Americans. Tribal members cooperated with each other for the common good and usually followed the tribe's code of behavior. Public disapproval, gossip, and loss of respect were effective punishments for breaking a rule of behavior. The threat of being publicly embarrassed in front of friends and family discouraged misbehavior.

In all tribes, however, legal problems sometimes arose. Two warriors might start a fight over an insult. A lazy man might steal his neighbor's food. Also, as in any society, there were always a few selfish people who would try to get around the laws of the tribe for personal gain.

In most tribes, a person who felt wronged sought to protect his or her own interests. It was acceptable in Native American societies for the victim of a crime (or his or her family) to confront the lawbreaker and demand justice. To reduce tensions, a chief or another respected person often stepped in and helped both sides come to an agreement. In most cases, the wrongdoer would admit guilt and compensate (make a payment to) the victim. Horses, food supplies, clothing, and tools were the usual forms of compensation. If an offender refused to pay the victim, a feud could erupt between the offender and the victim's family.

In cases where misconduct harmed the interests of the tribe, the punishment was decided by the chief, a tribal council, or even the family of the wrongdoer. For example, in some tribes killing a tribal member or violating a religious rule was thought to bring down a curse on the entire tribe. An offender was forced to make a payment to the victim or the victim's family or be kicked out of the tribe. (Imprisonment was rarely used as a punishment.) Many Native Americans, however, did not view offenses committed against outsiders as crimes. For example, stealing horses from another tribe or killing an enemy in battle were considered brave deeds.

In Native American societies, as in societies around the world, religion, custom, and law all offer guidance for individual behavior. Many religions have rules stating how a person should and should not act. Those who disobey a religious rule are believed to risk punishment or disapproval from a god or spirit. There is, however, usually no punishment for breaking a custom, other than disapproval.

On the other hand, people who disobey a law may often be punished. Societies authorize a certain person—such as a judge—or a certain group—such as a tribal council—to punish those people who break the law. For example, all societies have laws against murder. A person who kills another human being is usually judged and, if found guilty, punished for his or her crime. Often, laws also enforce religious rules of behavior, especially in societies that have a single, common religion.

Ceremonial clothing was worn by tribal chiefs and leaders.

Laws are important because they help people to live together. They let members of a society know what to expect from others and what others can expect from them. By using punishment to regulate unacceptable behavior, laws attempt to prevent conduct that might lead to conflicts between individuals or otherwise disrupt social order.

Tribal Law Today

Today, the U.S. government officially recognizes more than 500 Native American tribes. There are more than 1.5 million Native Americans living in the United States. About one quarter of them live on the country's 278 federal and state reservations. Many reservations face serious social problems, such as poverty, unemployment, and inadequate health care, housing, and education. Other Native Americans make their homes in cities. Los Angeles, San Francisco, Phoenix, Seattle, Tulsa, Denver, Albuquerque, and Minneapolis are just some of the large cities that have very sizable Native American populations.

About half of the tribes living in the United States have written constitutions that set forth the basic principles governing the tribe. These documents are modeled after the U.S. Constitution. Many tribes today have tribal governments that manage the internal affairs of the tribe, pass laws to ensure peace and order on the reservation, and negotiate with government agencies and other outsiders.

More than one hundred tribes have judicial systems that include tribal legal codes, tribal courts, and tribal police forces. Tribal courts handle minor crimes, known as misdemeanors, and disputes that occur on Native American lands. (Under U.S. law, serious crimes—such as murder—that occur on reservations are handled by U.S. federal courts.) Most tribal courts operate as local state courts do, except that there are no juries. Judges hear witnesses, evaluate

Tribal members often met in council to make decisions for their tribe.

evidence, and make decisions based on the tribal legal code. A person found guilty of a crime may be fined or imprisoned in a tribal jail.

A few tribes have courts that use traditional legal approaches to resolve disputes. The Seneca and the Navajo have peacemaker courts. Judges in these courts are well-respected community leaders. Using the traditional legal approaches of their tribe, peacemaker judges try to negotiate settlements between opposing sides by reaching a consensus. Several Pueblo tribes also have traditional courts that are conducted by religious leaders.

The following chapters examine tribal laws and legal traditions of Native Americans across North America.

Chapter

2

Plains Indians

Opposite:
Morgan Tosee, a
Comanche, performed
the men's traditional
warrior dance as part
of a program by the
American Indian
Dance Theatre in
April 1993. Among
Plains Indians,
successful warriors
were usually made
chiefs of their tribes.

The Great Plains of North America stretch from central
Texas to southern Canada and from the Mississippi River to
the Rocky Mountains. The eastern part of the plains, known
as the prairie, is mostly flat and treeless. High grasses, grow-
ing as tall as ten feet, once covered the prairie. The western
part of the plains, known as the Great Plains, has gently
rolling hills and was once covered with shorter grass.

 For thousands of years, many Native Americans traveled
across the plains. Some groups settled in the region, farming, hunting, and gathering food. Tribes that lived on the
prairie, such as the Pawnee and Mandan, mostly farmed.
They grew corn, squash, beans, and pumpkins and gathered
wild plants. They also hunted deer, elk, and sometimes
buffalo. The tribes that lived on the Great Plains—such as
the Sioux, Cheyenne, and Kiowa—hunted buffalo and
moved from place to place following the buffalo herds and
gathering wild plants.

17

✳

18

The way of life on the plains changed with the arrival of the horse, an animal that was not native to the Americas. Spanish explorers first brought horses to North America in the 1500s, but it was another 200 years before horses appeared on the plains. Plains Indians acquired horses both by trading with tribes from other regions and by raiding those tribes and taking their horses. The horse made it easier to hunt buffalo.

With the horse, hunters could chase buffalo and get closer to shoot their arrows. They also used horses to carry their belongings with them as they followed the buffalo herds. For many Plains Indians, including the tribes that had always farmed, life soon revolved around the buffalo. They ate buffalo meat and used buffalo hides to make clothing, storage containers, and coverings for their portable houses, known as tipis. Buffalo horns and bones were made into tools.

Because of the horse, Plains Indians had more food, clothing, and goods to trade than ever before. They also had more time for religious ceremonies. Both the religious beliefs and ceremonies of the Plains Indians stressed the importance of nature. They believed that spirits lived in all things—the sun, sky, land, water, animals, and plants. These spirits were seen as possessing a force that had a strong influence on human life. Plains tribes called this force by different names. The Sioux called it Wakan Tanka, while the Pawnee called it Tirarwa. Later, white people usually called it the Great Spirit.

The most important religious ceremony that was practiced on the plains was the Sun Dance, in which men slowly danced around a pole. These dancers often went into a trance and had religious visions. The ceremony gave thanks to all of the spirits that were believed to nourish the earth, provide enough food for the people, and protect the tribe from its enemies.

Members of the Cheyenne painted their bodies in preparation for participating in the Sun Dance.

With the horse, there was also more time—and cause—for warfare. Riding horseback, small raiding parties attacked other tribes. Warriors usually went on raids to gain honor for themselves, to get revenge against another tribe for an earlier attack, or merely to steal horses. Attackers would usually sneak up on an enemy camp and quietly ambush a few opponents. If the attackers were then detected by their enemies, hand-to-hand combat often followed. Some tribes began to fight against each other frequently, each side seeking revenge for the death of tribesmen in earlier attacks.

Traditional Law

The Plains Indians did not depend on written laws to govern themselves. Most tribes were very democratic, and everyone took part in tribal decisions. Chiefs—who were usually successful warriors or men respected for their wisdom—gave advice and provided leadership. In many tribes, the women chose the person who would become chief. They could remove the chief from his position if he lost the respect of the tribe or acted improperly. Chiefs who were responsible for tribal affairs were known as peace chiefs. Tribes also had war chiefs, who were always great warriors. War chiefs were in charge of raids and battles. In most tribes, the same person could not be both a peace chief and a war chief.

Chiefs did not have the authority to give orders or make decisions for the tribe by themselves. In most tribes, decisions or tribal matters were made by all the men in the tribe. When a problem arose, the men gathered in a meeting known as a council. Each man voiced his family's opinion. A final decision was made only when everyone at the council agreed on what action should be taken—that is, when a consensus had been reached. Because each family was represented at the meeting, the council's decision was respected

21

Red Cloud, seated second from left, was an Oglala Sioux chief in Montana. He signed the Treaty of Fort Laramie in 1868, which resulted in the withdrawal of the whites from Sioux lands.

by everyone in the tribe. For example, if the council decided that it was time to break camp and hunt buffalo, the tribe would do just that.

As might be expected, different tribes dealt with crimes and public disputes in different ways. In all tribes, however, there was a general desire for peace and harmony within the group. Whenever a conflict arose—whether it was a theft, a murder, or a feud between families—individuals in the tribe tried to find a solution that would satisfy everyone involved in the dispute. No one wanted a conflict to grow into a major blood feud in which rival families would seek revenge against each other in an endless cycle. Because tribes were small and many tribespeople were related to each other through marriages, a long-lasting feud could split families apart and destroy the tribe.

Sitting Bull was leader of the Hunkpapa Sioux. After the Battle of the Little Big Horn, he led his band to Canada.

✳

23

Order within a tribe depended a great deal on individuals following their own consciences. When a person did break one of their tribe's rules of behavior, he or she faced the disapproval and scorn of the other tribe members. Public disapproval was an effective punishment. By teasing, ignoring, or gossiping about the offender, everyone in the tribe could make life so difficult that he or she would quickly try to make things right.

The threat of public disapproval helped to discourage crime. Theft seldom occurred, for example, among the Cheyenne. When personal property was stolen and the thief was known, humiliation was the punishment. The victim might say to the thief in front of other tribe members, "If I had known you wanted the knife, I would have given it to you." Because sharing and giving gifts were qualities that were much admired among the Cheyenne, the victim would appear highly honorable and the thief would be publicly humiliated. The threat of embarrassing one's family or being shamed in front of friends kept most people from breaking their tribe's rules of behavior.

In most tribes, when crimes occurred, victims or their families sought justice from the wrongdoers themselves. Many legal conflicts, from theft to murder, were handled in this manner. In most cases, the offender admitted guilt and made some sort of payment to the victim. Horses, tools, and clothing were among items given to victims. The idea was to pay the victim for whatever damage that had been done so everyone could forgive, forget, and continue to live together in peace.

When those involved in a legal conflict did not agree on the payment, a chief, or an elder from a family not involved in the dispute, stepped in to work out a settlement. Sometimes a chief offered to pay part of the amount himself. The chief's involvement ensured that victims would accept the payment and that offenders would not think that they had been forced to pay too much.

The private settlement of legal conflicts worked well for most tribes. Among the Kiowa, for example, even a serious crime such as murder could be handled. If a murder occurred, the killer's family quickly sent gifts to the victim's family to discourage revenge. The killer stayed in the tipi of a priest, where he or she could not be harmed by the victim's family. To avoid a blood feud, a respected person who was not related to the killer or the victim brought the families together and helped them agree on how much the victim's family should be paid for their loss.

Native Americans had ideas about property use that were different from many non-Native Americans. Plains Indians believed that everyone could use the land and its natural resources freely. All tribes could hunt, camp, and plant crops wherever they wished. No tribe or person was thought of as the owner of a parcel of land.

This quilled, buckskin vest was made by a Sioux man. Among many Plains tribes, a man's property was passed on to his sons when he died.

★

25

People did own their personal belongings, such as clothing, tools, and tipis. Sharing, however, was common among Plains Indians. No one minded if another person borrowed tools, cookware, and similar items. A dispute might arise, though, if an item was not returned or if the borrower was careless with it. In these cases, the owner might confront the borrower and demand the return or replacement of his or her property. Many tribes also felt there was a difference between taking an item during the daytime, which was considered borrowing, and taking an item at night or by sneaky means, which was considered stealing.

In most Plains tribes, when a man died, his belongings—such as bows, arrows, and horses—were usually passed down to his sons. When a woman died, her belongings—such as bowls and farming tools—were passed down to her daughters. Among the Cheyenne, however, a dead person's things, except for horses, were given to people outside the family. When a Comanche died, his or her things were destroyed. The Comanche believed that a dead person's belongings then went with him or her into the afterlife.

In every Plains tribe, murder was a very serious offense. Among the Comanche, the family of a murder victim sought revenge, and family members did not rest until the murderer had been killed. Most often, the killer's family accepted that the killing of a murderer was just and did not then seek revenge for that death. Among the Crow and most other Plains tribes, however, the victim's family did not seek revenge by killing. Instead, the victim's family expected the killer to make compensation in horses, tools, and clothing. Sometimes the killer took care of the victim's family for the rest of his or her life.

The Cheyenne handled murders in another way. They considered murder a crime against the whole tribe, not a private matter to be settled between the killer and the family

of the victim. The Cheyenne believed that a murder made the spirits unhappy and that the spirits would curse the tribe. A murder could cause bad luck in hunting and warfare and could prevent rainfall or cause floods.

When a murder occurred, the Cheyenne tribal council, known as the Council of Forty-four, met immediately. If the forty-four peace chiefs who sat on the council determined that the accused was guilty, they told the killer to leave the tribe. By sending the killer away, the council prevented the victim's family from seeking revenge. This way, family was not set against family and peace in the tribe was maintained. After the killer left the tribe, a shaman (a religious leader) held a religious ceremony to cleanse the tribe of the murder.

Being exiled from a Plains Indian tribe was a very serious punishment. It might mean starvation or death at the hands of an unfriendly tribe. Sometimes a friendly tribe, such as the Arapaho, permitted a Cheyenne who had been banished to come and live with them, but he or she would be treated as an outsider. After five or ten years, the person who had been sent away could ask the Cheyenne Council of Forty-four for permission to rejoin the tribe. If the victim's family did not object, the banished individual could return.

Among the Cheyenne and other Plains tribes, hunter societies, which were in charge of the buffalo hunt, had legal duties. During the summer months, when the tribe camped together, hunter societies made sure that no one acted selfishly. If someone attacked the herd before everyone was ready, the buffalo could escape and the people could go hungry. The hunter societies punished those who broke the rules of the hunt by taking away their horses, not giving them any buffalo meat, or even by whipping them.

Plains Indians Today

Today, many Plains Indians live on reservations throughout the Great Plains. There are Cheyenne reservations in Montana and Oklahoma, a Crow reservation in eastern Montana, a Kiowa reservation in Oklahoma, and Sioux reservations in North and South Dakota, Minnesota, and Montana. Plains Indians also live in cities, such as Rapid City, South Dakota, and Denver, Colorado.

Some Plains tribes—including the Cheyenne, Crow, and Sioux—have written constitutions, tribal governments, and tribal court systems. The tribal courts of the Oglala Sioux, for example, handle about 3,000 cases each year. Tribal court judges follow the Oglala Sioux tribal code, which is a set of written laws similar to U.S. legal codes. The judges also try to consider Sioux legal traditions in making their final decisions. For example, a Sioux found guilty of theft will usually be fined instead of sent to jail; for imprisonment is not a traditional punishment among the Sioux. In resolving disputes that occur within the tribe, the judges try to make decisions that benefit the whole community.

The Tribes of the West

Historically, Native American groups in the western part of North America have been many and varied. More than one hundred tribes lived in what is now California. The Pacific Northwest, which stretched from present-day northern California to present-day southern Alaska, was home to many successful tribes. In the Plateau region—which included what is now southwestern Canada, Montana, Idaho, eastern Washington, and eastern Oregon—tribes lived in villages along river banks. Several small tribes scratched out a living in the deserts of the Great Basin, which included what is now eastern California, southeastern Oregon, southern Idaho, western Colorado, western Wyoming, Nevada, and Utah.

Because of its mild weather and plentiful natural resources, California had a very large population of Native Americans. Scientists estimate that as many as 310,000 Native Americans lived in California when Columbus sailed to the Americas in 1492. In the north, tribes lived on the coast of the Pacific Ocean and along rivers inland. Fish was

*Opposite:
Pioneers saw many opportunities in settling the West. In the process, however, they permanently changed the lives of the Native Americans who lived there.*

the main source of food for these tribes, which included the Hoopa and Shasta. In central California, the Miwok, Pomo, and other tribes hunted, fished, and gathered plants. About three fifths of California tribes lived in the central region. In southern California, some tribes, such as the Chumash, lived along the coast and fished. Farther south, small tribes now known as the Mission Indians lived in the desert. They survived by hunting small game and gathering plants.

Many California tribes relied heavily on acorns and other plants for food. Women ground the acorns into a type of flour, which was used to make bread or porridge. Most tribes gathered shellfish or hunted deer and small game, such as rabbits, squirrels, porcupines, ducks, and geese. California tribes also collected local resources, such as salt, seaweed, and obsidian—a black stone used to make arrowheads, knives, and axes. They traded these items to tribes from other regions, where these materials were not available.

The family was the basis of social life within California tribes. Groups of related families lived together in villages.

These tools were used by members of the Inupiat Nation in Kotzebue, Alaska.

Some of these villages had about fifty people. Others had several hundred. Several larger villages had as many as 2,000 people. Men served as village leaders. They gave advice, organized hunting parties, and settled minor disputes.

California tribes believed in supreme beings who created the universe and controlled all life on Earth. In some tribes, a supreme being was thought to be an animal figure. These California Native Americans believed that everything in the universe had a spiritual power. Dances and ceremonies were held to offer thanks and give prayers to these powers. The Salmon Dance was held in spring, for example, and the Acorn Feast was held in autumn.

The mild, rainy climate of the Northwest Coast region—which included the western parts of what is now Oregon, Washington, and British Columbia—provided many natural resources. Northwest Coast tribes gathered berries and a variety of foods in the forests, fished the rivers for salmon and other fish, and trapped sea otters. In summer, they lived in temporary villages close to their sources of food. In winter, they lived in permanent villages, spending much of their time in religious ceremonies and dances.

Most Northwest Coast tribes, including the Haida, Chinook, and Kwakiutl, lived comfortable lives. Each family had a specific rank, which depended on its wealth. Some families had many belongings and high social positions. Other families had fewer belongings and lower standings in society. Family members worked hard to add to the family fortunes so the family could improve its rank in the tribe.

Families showed their wealth by hosting a potlatch, a large party that included feasting, speech making, and dancing. The host family gave its guests gifts, including canoes, blankets, and tools. By giving away many gifts, families demonstrated their wealth and could improve their rank in the tribe. Potlatches were held to celebrate many events,

Wishham fishermen used long spears to catch fish. Some Northwest clans claimed specific fishing places as their very own.

including births and deaths in the family, the building of a new house, and the winning of a battle.

Not much is known about the religion of Northwest Coast tribes because they did not keep written records. Like most Native Americans, however, they believed that spirits were deeply involved in everyday life. Northwest Coast tribes held many religious ceremonies to honor the spirits. Every Kwakiutl, for example, belonged to a dancing society. During ceremonies, dancers wore elaborate masks as they acted out tribal legends and family histories. They also used magic tricks and special effects to heighten the emotion of these dances.

In the Plateau region, most Native Americans lived in small villages located along riverbanks. They fished and hunted deer, mountain sheep, elk, and rabbit. They added to their diet by gathering such foods as wild onions, carrots, nuts, and berries. They built canoes to travel on rivers, which served as trading routes. Once horses arrived in the region, Plateau tribes became known for their skill at riding the large, swift animals.

Tribes that lived in the Plateau region included the Nez Perce, Flathead, and Walla Walla. Most tribes were governed by a headman. These chiefs had limited powers and often held meetings with tribe members to discuss issues that affected the whole group.

Plateau tribes believed in a supernatural power that touched all living things. They called upon the spirits to provide plenty of game animals and plants. Shamans were thought to have special powers, such as curing illnesses and making contact with the spirit world. Individuals also had personal guardian spirits that protected them and helped them defeat an enemy. To find a guardian spirit, young men and women went on vision quests, which often involved some endurance of pain. Bathing in ice-cold streams or not eating for days were common ways of summoning a vision of one's guardian spirit.

Life was difficult for Native Americans living in the Great Basin region, with its hot summers and cold winters. Food and water were hard to find in the dry deserts, mountains, and canyons of the region. Great Basin tribes ate nuts, seeds, berries, and roots. They also caught and ate insects, snakes, lizards, and rabbits. Because natural resources were scarce, the region was not heavily populated.

Great Basin tribes, such as the Shoshone and Paiute, were organized into small family units. These small groups, ranging from one family to thirty people, moved constantly in search of food and water. Each group was led by the male head of the family.

Many religious beliefs and ceremonies of the Plateau tribes were related to the most important activity of the people—finding food and water. The Native Americans in this region asked spirits for help and guidance in finding food. They considered water to be sacred.

Traditional Law

Among all the tribes of the West, crimes and disputes were handled privately by individuals. They were not considered matters for tribal review. The injured person, or his or her family members, sought payment when they felt wronged. Often, a chief or elder was chosen to help settle disputes, such as a fight between hostile neighbors, but his duties ended when the situation was resolved. As among Plains tribes, disapproval and gossip were the primary means for punishing those who broke the tribe's rules of behavior.

Among California tribes, murder was compensated by payment of strings of shells to the relatives of the victim. If the offender did not make this payment, the victim's family was likely to seek revenge by killing the murderer. Among the Plateau tribes, such as the Nez Perce, a killer was also expected to make a payment to the family of the victim. Payment was usually in the form of canoes, animal pelts, or food supplies. Horses later became the major form of payment.

Individuals in the tribes of the West did not own land. For the most part, these tribes believed that all people were free to fish, hunt, and grow crops wherever they wanted. Some California tribes, however, such as the Pomo, did claim the right to fish in a certain section of the river or to gather acorns from a particular section of the forest.

Buckskin Charlie was chief of the Ute tribe at the turn of the twentieth century.

Among Northwest Coast tribes, groups of related people, known as clans, claimed the right to specific fishing and gathering places. These places were considered possessions of the clan headman. If a person from another clan fished or gathered food from these places, a feud between the clans might develop. Feuds also arose over other rights controlled by headmen. The headman of a clan could give someone in his clan the right to be called by a certain name, to use a specific design in tattoos or house decorations, or to perform a particular dance or wear a particular mask. If a person from the Raven Clan, for example, performed one of the dances of the Wolf Clan, a feud would break out between the two groups.

In some Northwest Coast tribes, wealthy families owned slaves. Most of the slaves were women and children of other tribes who had been captured during wars and raids. The slaves performed various chores, such as cleaning houses. Because slaves were thought of as property and not as humans, they had no rights. A slave owner could even kill a slave without being punished.

Tribes of the West Today

With the arrival of Europeans in the West, many tribes were completely wiped out and many of the traditions of the surviving peoples were destroyed. The California tribes suffered the most. Only a few survived. Today, some California Native Americans live on reservations, but most have adopted American lifestyles and live in cities, particularly Los Angeles, San Francisco, Oakland, and Long Beach.

Many of the traditional ways of the western tribes—including their languages, religious beliefs, and their legal traditions—have been lost forever. Most of these Native Americans live in cities such as Seattle, Washington; Portland, Oregon; Vancouver, British Columbia; Salt Lake City,

These Nez Perce men participated in a powwow in 1950. Even though their ways of life have changed, many Native Americans have kept a lot of their tribal traditions alive.

Utah; and Reno, Nevada. A few tribes live on reservations. Many Shoshone make their homes on reservations in Utah, Wyoming, Idaho, and Nevada. There are Paiute reservations in Utah, Nevada, and Oregon; Nez Perce reservations in Washington and Idaho; and a Walla Walla reservation in Oregon. Some Northwest Coast tribes live on reservations in the Canadian province of British Columbia (the Haida, Kwakiutl, and many others) and in the state of Washington (the Chinook).

Some larger tribes, such as the Shoshone, Nez Perce, and Ute, have written constitutions, tribal governments, and tribal court systems. The tribal courts are very much like other U.S. courts. Judges wear robes, witnesses testify, evidence is presented, and verdicts are announced. Although many tribal legal traditions have been lost over the years, the judges in tribal courts try to use tribal legal traditions in making their decisions.

Chapter

4

Southwest Tribes

Many different Native American groups lived in the Southwest before the Spanish explorers reached the area in the sixteenth century. The region, which includes the present-day states of Arizona and New Mexico, is a land of striking beauty. The region's rivers have carved deep canyons, including the Grand Canyon, into the earth. Forests of pine, juniper, and other evergreens cover the craggy mountains. Flat-topped mesas rise high above the flatlands. The Southwest is also a dry land. Only a few inches of rain fall in the region each year.

Most Southwest tribes made their living by farming or raiding. The Pueblo people—such as the Hopi, Zuni, and Acoma—were farmers. They lived in villages located on top of mesas. (The name Pueblo comes from the Spanish word for "town." It refers to the farming groups who lived in what is now New Mexico.) Their houses were made of stone and mud or from adobe bricks, which were made from mud and straw and dried in the sun. The thick walls kept

Opposite:
Pueblo villages dotted with adobe homes are still seen today in Laguna Pueblo, New Mexico.

39

Hopi kachina dolls were used to teach children about tribal beliefs.

the houses warm in winter and cool in summer. Sometimes adobe houses were connected to each other both in rows and on top of one another. The farmers grew their crops in fields located close to their villages.

Water was important to the farmers of the Southwest. Because there was little rainfall, the tribes built ditches to bring water from the rivers to their fields. These irrigation ditches also brought water from reservoirs that trapped rainfall. The men worked hard in the fields—planting corn, beans, squash, cotton, and tobacco. Corn was the most important crop.

These Native Americans used ground corn to make corn mush, tortillas, and piñole (a drink made from corn and water). They harvested corn-stalks to make bedding and used cornmeal and corn pollen in religious ceremonies.

The Navajo and Apache had a different way of life than that of the Pueblo people. They gathered wild plants, such as acorns, cactus fruits, and nuts. They used bows and arrows to hunt deer, antelope, and mountain sheep and traps to catch rabbits and prairie dogs. Both Navajo and Apache women grew crops in small gardens.

When they did not have enough to eat, the Navajo and the Apache survived by raiding the farming tribes. They sneaked into Pueblo villages to steal food, clothing, fire-wood, and other supplies. If detected, the raiders fought to the death. Apache men were daring warriors and the most feared raiders in the Southwest. They often engaged in warfare, usually to avenge the death of fellow Apaches in earlier raids.

Native Americans in the Southwest were deeply religious. They held religious rituals throughout the year. In such ceremonies as the Rain Dance and the Corn Dance, they asked the spirits to bring rain and gave thanks for the harvest. Religion was a part of almost every aspect of life. Prayers were offered whenever there was a birth, a marriage, or a death.

Many special ceremonies and dances were performed in the village plaza, or public square. Among the Hopi and some other Pueblo groups, masked dancers known as kachinas performed at important ceremonies. Some kachinas represented the rain gods, which were very important to these farming peoples. Parents gave their children small dolls carved out of wood that were painted and dressed to look like the kachinas. These dolls helped teach young Pueblo children about the many different rain gods in which they believed.

Kachina dancers from the Hopi tribe are represented in this painting by artist Riley Quoyavema.

Some religious ceremonies were held in kivas—underground chambers where men met to pray and boys learned their tribal traditions. Women and girls were not allowed to enter kivas.

The Navajo and the Apache adopted many of the religious beliefs and ceremonies of the Pueblo people. There were many holy people in the Navajo religion, including Changing Woman, who gave corn to the ancestors of the Navajo, and Spider Woman, who taught the Navajo how to weave. The Apache also believed in a number of different spirits, such as the Mountain Spirits. They held dances and festivals to honor all of these powerful forces.

Traditional Law

The Pueblo believed that the world was in perfect balance, but that this balance could easily be damaged. Any behavior that upset the balance of nature—even arguing, lying, or cheating—threatened the welfare of the entire village. When the natural order was disturbed, crops could fail, people could get sick, and rain clouds, with their precious water for crops, could blow away. Most of the rules of behavior in Pueblo society were aimed at making sure that no one upset the balance of nature.

Religion had a very strong influence on the laws of the Pueblo. Each village was led by a priest, who was guided by the spirits. The priest made sure that disputes and violations of village laws were settled quickly. Those who broke religious rules, or even asked the spirits to harm another person, were ordered by the priest to leave the village.

The Navajo lived in small bands that roamed the deserts looking for food and raiding farming villages. A headman led each local band. Although the Navajo headman was not a religious leader, this tribe believed that the headman received his power directly from the spirits. The headman's opinions on tribal matters were influential, but he usually sought the advice of elders and shamans before making decisions.

The Apache, like the Navajo, had no central government. Roving bands, composed of related people, followed a headman. Apache headmen were usually successful warriors. They were highly respected, but had no power to make or enforce laws. Although the Apache were merciless toward rival tribes, they had a strong sense of community and were generous to members of their own tribe.

Native Americans in the Southwest usually did not violate tribal laws. They feared that the spirits would punish them even for minor offenses, such as lying and cheating. Major crimes of violence and public disputes rarely occurred. When they did, the parties involved quickly settled the matter. Offenders and their relatives compensated victims with gifts of personal property.

Ownership of land was unknown to the Navajo and Apache. In Pueblo society, the fields were divided among separate families. Women were the heads of the families, and they owned the house, land, crops, herds, and household goods. When a woman died, her property was passed down to her daughters and granddaughters. When a man died, his belongings, such as masks and costumes used in religious ceremonies, were passed down to his sons and grandsons. Some men and women may have been buried with the materials and tools they used when they were living.

As in all Native American societies, murder was a serious offense in the Southwest. Among the Hopi, Navajo, and Apache, a murder led to blood revenge. The family of the victim set out to kill the murderer or a member of his or her family. Among the Pueblo (except for the Hopi), the victim's family did not seek the death of the killer. Instead, the killer had to pay the victim's family.

Southwest Tribes Today

Spanish explorers, looking for gold, arrived in the Southwest in the mid-1500s. Spanish missionaries soon followed, hoping to convert Native Americans to Christianity. The missionaries forced many Southwest Native Americans to give up their religion, to build churches, and to grow crops that were sold in Mexico and Europe. The Spanish treated them as slaves. In the 1800s, white settlers from the United States moved into the region, claiming much of the land as their own.

Ruins of the Pecos Mission Church remain in Pecos Pueblo, New Mexico. During the Pueblo Revolt, Spanish colonists were driven from their lands.

Today, there are about 40,000 Pueblo people. Many live on the nineteen Pueblo reservations in New Mexico, such as Zuni, Acoma, Taos, and Santa Clara. Each reservation now has a governor, who is responsible for all the tribal dealings with the outside world. Most reservations have a tribal council, which is usually made up of previous governors. Pueblo shamans still have a great deal of power, however. Each shaman is in charge of religious life in his village. The shaman also chooses the governor and gives him important advice on village matters.

Most pueblos now have written constitutions, tribal police, and tribal courts. These tribal courts operate very much like the tribal courts in other regions. A few pueblos, however,—such as Jemez, Zia, and Santa Ana—have more traditional forms of government. The governor handles most criminal cases and disputes between individuals, following the old ways. These pueblos also have traditional judicial bodies known as religious courts. Because these courts act in secret, not much is known about them.

The Navajo tribe is now the second largest tribal group in the United States. Their reservation, located in northeast Arizona and parts of New Mexico and Utah, is the largest in the country. A tribal council, consisting of eighty delegates, governs the Navajo. The council makes decisions for the tribe and enacts laws to govern it. The Navajo have a tribal court system that includes a juvenile court and a supreme court. Navajo courts interpret and enforce laws, resolve disputes between people, and settle issues between the tribal government and the members of the tribe.

In 1982, the Navajo tribal council created peacemaker courts. Peacemaker judges are usually respected leaders in the community. They are appointed and supervised by district court judges. The peacemaker judges try to use traditional Navajo methods to resolve community disputes.

Chapter

5

Tribes of the Eastern Woodlands

The Eastern Woodlands of North America were home to many Native Americans. The region extended from the Atlantic Ocean to Texas and from the Great Lakes to the Gulf of Mexico. The landscape of this larger territory had many different features—beaches, gently rolling hills, mountains, lakes, river valleys, marshes, and swamps.

The dense forests throughout the East provided tribes with many resources. Native Americans used wood from trees to make homes, canoes, and tools. Wood was also used in fires for cooking and for warmth. Tree bark was used to make clothing, roofs, and bedding. The animals that lived in the forests provided food and clothing.

Native Americans who lived in the northern part of the Eastern Woodlands were mainly hunters and gatherers. Men in the northern tribes—such as the Iroquois, Delaware, Ojibwa (also called Chippewa), Huron, and Algonquin— used bows and arrows to hunt deer, moose, beavers, otters, and other animals. They also trapped or hunted small game,

Opposite:
This painting, called the "Ancient Creek Ceremonial Figure," was painted by artist Joan Hill.

such as squirrels, rabbits, raccoons, opossums, and wild turkeys. Disputes over hunting grounds often led to wars between tribes. Tribes often raided each other to get revenge for the deaths of tribespeople or to steal supplies.

In many of these hunting tribes, women were the farmers. Corn, beans, pumpkins, and squash were their major crops. Northern tribes also gathered wild plants, berries, fruits, and nuts. They fished in rivers, streams, lakes, and the Atlantic Ocean, and coastal tribes gathered shellfish, such as oysters and clams.

In the southern part of the eastern region, the climate was warmer and wetter. Most southern tribes—such as the Cherokee, Seminole, and Creek—were mainly farmers. As in the North, women were in charge of the farming. They grew many crops, including corn, squash, sweet potatoes, beans, peas, cabbage, melons, and tobacco. Tobacco was a sacred crop that was used in many religious rituals. Women also gathered wild plants, nuts, and berries.

Using spears, bow and arrows, blowguns, and traps, men in southern tribes hunted deer and small game. They also caught fish with spears, traps, and nets. When they were not hunting, men spent much of their time preparing for, and fighting in, wars.

Most Eastern Woodlands tribes lived in villages located near rivers, streams, lakes, or the ocean. Northern tribes lived in villages close to their fields. Some of the people often left these villages in order to hunt during certain seasons. Southern tribes lived in their villages year-round. Many of these villages had large populations because the women could grow enough food to feed many people. Most Native Americans in the South led comfortable lives.

Many Eastern Woodlands tribes were organized into clans, which are groups of related families who are all descended from a common ancestor. Each clan usually had an

animal—such as a beaver, deer, or bear—as its clan symbol.
In most tribes, men and women in the same clan could not
marry each other. Among the Iroquois tribes, families from
the same clan lived together in longhouses. These buildings
were between fifty and one hundred feet in length.

Eastern Woodlands tribes had different ways of governing themselves. Many northern tribes had peace chiefs and
war chiefs. Peace chiefs, known as sachems, were responsible for handling village affairs. Sachem also refers to a
ruler or chief of allied tribes. A council of elders gave the
sachems advice on tribal matters. Sachems were elected by
women elders. If the tribe lost confidence in the sachem's
abilities to lead, the women would vote for a new peace
chief. War chiefs were usually skilled warriors. They were
also responsible for organizing war parties and protecting
villages. The sachem among the Wampanoags, in the
present-day state of Massachusetts, served as a ruler or chief
of allied tribes.

Some southern tribes, such as the Cherokee, also had
peace chiefs and war chiefs. The peace chiefs, called white
chiefs in some tribes, were in charge of maintaining order in
their villages. They helped make decisions, such as what
crops to plant, and helped settle disputes between individuals, families, and clans. Matters of importance were decided
by village councils, which were composed of the men in the
tribe. War chiefs, called red chiefs in some tribes, gave
advice concerning warfare and raids.

The Natchez, a tribe that lived along the Mississippi
River in what are now the states of Mississippi and Louisi-
ana, were divided into social classes. A royal family stood at
the top of the social order. Like monarchs in Europe, the
chief of the Natchez, known as the Great Sun, had total
power over his subjects. The Great Sun wore a crown made
of swan feathers and sat on a throne made of goose feathers.

Just below the royal family was a group of nobles known as the Suns. These people held positions of power in war parties and in Natchez villages. Underneath the Suns was a group known as the Honored Men and Women. They were less powerful nobles. At the bottom of the social order was a group of commoners called the Stinkards. They did the farming and all the other hard work.

Religion was central to the daily lives of the Native Americans who lived in the Eastern Woodlands. All things in the universe—plants, animals, rocks, rivers, the sun, moon, and stars—were seen as part of the sacred cycle of life. Eastern Native Americans taught their children to respect all living things, which were believed to have souls. They believed that a great power created the world and controlled their own lives. They performed ceremonies to give thanks to the creator of life for their harvests and to ask that the gifts from the creator continue in the future. Singing, drumming, and dancing were part of these ceremonies.

Traditional Law

In many Eastern Woodlands tribes, theft, murder, and other crimes rarely occurred. Each member of a tribe had a sense of duty to the community. Breaking the tribal rules would disturb the harmony of the village. The threat of embarrassing one's clan and losing the respect of others in the tribe discouraged most people from committing crimes or getting into arguments.

Whenever a crime did occur, it was customary for the victim to face the offender and demand justice. In most cases, the wrongdoer admitted guilt and made some sort of payment to the victim, such as food, supplies, or tools. In larger tribes, such as the Cherokee and the five tribes of the Iroquois nation, the victim's clan chief and offender's clan chief sometimes settled legal disputes. If a crime or an

Payment, such as this Creek beaded shoulder bag, was made to crime victims in Eastern Woodland societies.

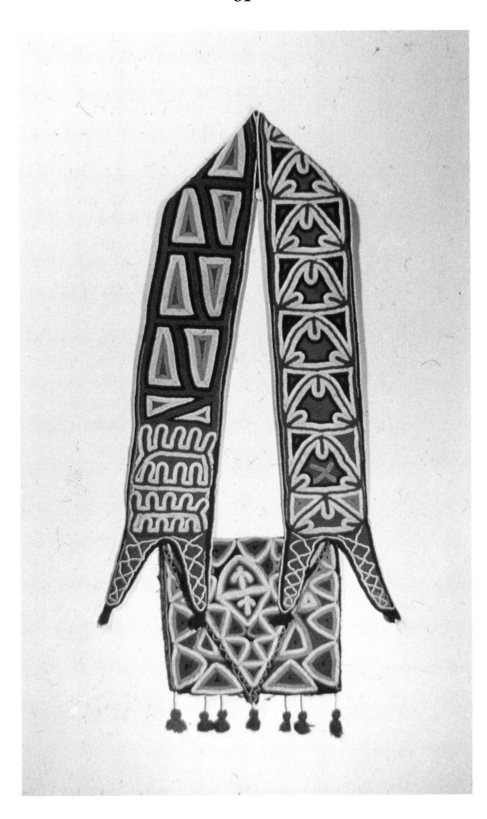

argument erupted into a clash between two clans, a chief from a third clan stepped in to help both sides reach a fair settlement.

In cases where a person's misbehavior was thought to harm the entire tribe, punishment was decided by a chief, a tribal council, or even the family of the wrongdoer. Usually, the offender was forced to compensate the victim. Those who broke tribal laws regularly were exiled from the tribe or the village.

Eastern Woodlands tribes believed that the land and its natural resources could be used by anyone, but families and clans claimed the plots of land that they farmed. Food and household items were privately owned, but everyone was expected to share. If there was a theft, the owner sought to recover his or her belongings and humiliate the thief in public.

Because women were the farmers in Eastern Woodlands tribes, they were considered the owners of the farmland and farming tools. When a woman died, her land and tools were passed down to her daughters or other women in her clan. When a man died, his belongings, such as bows, arrows, and war clubs, were passed down to his sons and other men in his clan. Men and women were also buried with materials and tools that they owned when they were living.

In some Eastern Woodlands tribes, such as the Iroquois, murder was a matter to be settled by the village council. The council decided exactly what payment the killer should make to the victim's family. In other tribes, however, murder was considered an offense against the victim's entire clan. Among the Cherokee, for example, murder usually called for revenge, which required no less than the death of the murderer. If the murderer could not be caught, the men in the victim's clan eventually killed another member of the murderer's clan.

Cornplanter was a war captain of the Seneca tribe and belonged to the Iroquois League. This painting shows Cornplanter in 1796.

Some Eastern Woodlands tribes joined together in confederacies to protect themselves from attack by neighboring tribes. The Abenaki Confederacy included several tribes that lived in the Northeast, such as the Penobscot, Passamaquoddy, and Micmac. The Ojibwa, Ottawa, and Potawatomi also formed a confederacy, which they called the Three Fires. The Three Fires Confederacy was located in the Great Lakes area. In what is now present-day Virginia, 32 tribes and 200 villages united into the powerful Powhatan Confederacy.

✱

The largest Native American confederacy was the League of the Iroquois. Two men, Deganawidah and Hiawatha, brought the five Iroquois tribes together. The Mohawk, Oneida, Onondaga, Cayuga, and Seneca formed a confederacy known as the Iroquois Confederacy or the Iroquois League. This confederacy formed in the late 1500s and is still located in the present-day state of New York. The tribes agreed to stop fighting among themselves and to live together in peace. They also decided to combine their forces to defend each other against outside enemies.

Each of the five tribes continued to govern its own territory. Also, every autumn all five tribes sent representatives to the Grand Council of the league. The Grand Council, which met at the village of Onondaga, consisted of fifty sachems and pine tree chiefs, who were appointed because of their wisdom or achievements. The Grand Council discussed matters that concerned all five tribes.

The Grand Council declared war, made peace, and entered into treaties with other tribes. It could not make a final decision unless all five tribes agreed on a course of action. The League of the Iroquois became a strong confederacy. At the height of its power, it controlled territory stretching from New England to the Mississippi River.

The constitution of the League of the Iroquois was known as the Great Law of Peace. This constitution was written on wampum belts. Wampum belts are sashes of small beads made from seashells arranged in meaningful patterns. They were used in the Grand Council to recite the Great Law of Peace. The Great Law of Peace was the first constitution in North America.

During the American Revolution (1775–1783), the leaders of the new United States—such as George Washington, Benjamin Franklin, and Thomas Jefferson—looked to the League of the Iroquois as a model for a federation of states. Like the five Iroquois tribes, the thirteen original colonies joined together to form a nation while still keeping control over state governments. Like the sachems who represented their respective tribes, members of the U.S. Congress represent their states. Also, just as Iroquois representatives met for the Grand Council in Onondaga to decide matters for the league, the representatives of each state meet in Washington, D.C., to decide matters of law and government for the United States.

Eastern Woodlands Tribes Today

Native Americans living in the Eastern Woodlands region were among the first in what is now the United States to have contact with Europeans and to suffer the effects of European settlement. Some Eastern Woodlands tribes did not survive long after the arrival of Europeans. The tribes that did survive lost many people to war, disease, and starvation. In the process, many tribal traditions were lost.

Although many Native Americans now live west of the Mississippi River, some still make their homes in the eastern United States. There are several large Native American communities in New York City; Buffalo, New York; Milwaukee, Wisconsin; Montreal, Canada; and other eastern cities. There are also small reservations in the North, such as the Seneca reservations in New York, the Mohawk reservations in New York and Canada, and the Ojibwa reservations in Michigan and Wisconsin.

In the 1800s, the U.S. government forced many Native Americans in the South to move to the West. Today, many Eastern tribes—including the Cherokee, Creek, and Seminole—live in Oklahoma and other western states. There are some reservations in the South, most notably the Cherokee reservation in North Carolina and two Seminole reservations in Florida.

CONSTITUTION

OF THE

CHEROKEE NATION,

MADE AND ESTABLISHED

AT A

GENERAL CONVENTION OF DELEGATES,

DULY AUTHORISED FOR THAT PURPOSE.

AT

NEW ECHOTA,

JULY 26, 1827.

━━━━━━

PRINTED FOR THE CHEROKEE NATION,
AT THE OFFICE OF THE STATESMAN AND PATRIOT,
GEORGIA.

The cover of the constitution of the Cherokee nation. In 1827, this tribe created a new government.

Some Eastern Woodlands tribes, such as the Cherokee, have created their own constitutions, tribal governments, and tribal court systems. In 1827, the Cherokee set up a whole new system of tribal government. The rules for this government were contained in a constitution that was modeled after the U.S. Constitution.

Since 1840, some legal disputes among the Seneca have been resolved in peacemaker courts. These courts handle disputes between tribe members. They do not hear criminal cases. Peacemaker judges, who are elected by the tribal council, use traditional Seneca methods to resolve conflicts. They try to help the two sides come to an agreement that satisfies everyone. The final decision in the case is made by the parties themselves, not by the judges. Peacemaker courts recall the old ways of the Seneca. Unlike modern courts, where one party is blamed for a dispute and punished by the court, peacemaker courts bring tribe members together to resolve disputes and restore harmony in the community.

Glossary

adobe A kind of brick made from mud and straw that is dried in the sun. Native Americans of the Southwest used adobe to make their houses.

anthropologist A scientist who studies human beings and the different ways in which they live.

clan A social group within a tribe that is made up of several families who are descended from a common ancestor.

confederacy A political union of several tribes that join together for a common purpose.

custom A way of acting that has become accepted by a society.

kachina One of hundreds of supernatural beings that many Pueblo believe live in the American Southwest. Wooden dolls of the kachinas are given to Pueblo children to teach them about these important spirits.

kiva An underground chamber where men in Southwest tribes gather to conduct religious ceremonies and boys learn tribal traditions.

law A rule of behavior that, when violated, results in punishment by an authorized representative of society.

potlatch A ceremony held by the Tlingit, Kwakiutl, and other Northwest Coast tribes. At a potlatch, the hosts offered their relatives and friends costly food and gifts to display their wealth and their power within their village.

powwow A conference or gathering of Native Americans; often characterized by feasts, dancing, and celebration.

pueblo Native American village made of large clay-brick dwellings. The many Southwest tribes that have lived in these types of houses, such as the Hopi and the Zuni, are known as the Pueblo.

reservation A tract of land set aside by the United States for a group of Native Americans. Usually, reservations were small plots of poor-quality land offered to Native Americans only after white settlers had seized their lands.

sachem A peace chief who was responsible for handling village affairs. Sachem also refers to a ruler or chief of allied tribes.

shaman A religious leader who cures illnesses and makes contact with the spirit world. Shamans are also known as medicine men.

tipi A cone-shaped portable house made from a large animal-hide cover and a frame of wooden poles. Plains Indians decorated their tipis with paint.

treaty A written agreement made between two groups of people. The Native Americans of North America signed many treaties with the United States and Canada. These governments often broke the promises they made to various Native American groups.

tribe A group of Native American people who share the same religious, cultural, and social beliefs.

Further Reading

D'Apice, Mary. *The Pueblo*. Vero Beach, FL: Rourke, 1990.

Doherty, Craig A., and Katherine M. Doherty. *The Apaches and the Navajos*. New York: Franklin Watts, 1991.

_____. *The Crow*. Vero Beach, FL: Rourke, 1994.

_____. *The Huron*. Vero Beach, FL: Rourke, 1994.

_____. *The Ute*. Vero Beach, FL: Rourke, 1994.

Grant, Bruce. *Concise Encyclopedia of the American Indian*. Avenal, NJ: Outlet Book, 1989.

McCall, Barbara. *The Iroquois*. Vero Beach, FL: Rourke, 1989.

Prentzas, G.S. *The Kwakiutl*. New York: Chelsea House, 1993.

Stan, Susan. *The Navajo*. Vero Beach, FL: Rourke, 1989.

Tomchek, Ann Heinrichs. *The Hopi*. Chicago: Childrens Press, 1992.

Warren, Scott. *Cities in the Sand: The Ancient Civilizations of the Southwest*. San Francisco: Chronicle Books, 1992.

Wolfson, Evelyn. *From Abenaki to Zuni: A Dictionary of Native American Tribes*. New York: Walker, 1988.

Index

Photo Credits
Cover: ©British Museum; p. 6: ©Craig J. Brown/Liaison International; pp. 10, 13, 15, 19, 21, 32, 35, 53: Library of Congress; p. 16: ©Theo Westenberger/Gamma Liaison; pp. 22, 41, 46, 51, 56: ©Blackbirch Press, Inc.; p. 24: ©Tom McHugh/ Photo Researchers, Inc.; pp. 26, 30: ©Lawrence Migdale/Photo Researchers, Inc.; pp. 28, 38, 44: ©North Wind Picture Archives; p. 37: National Park Service/Nez Perce National Historical Park; p. 40: ©Day Williams/Photo Researchers, Inc.